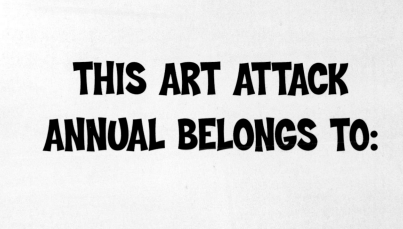

THIS ART ATTACK ANNUAL BELONGS TO:

£7.99

LET'S HAVE AN ART ATTACK

WELCOME TO THE ART ATTACK ANNUAL 2005, WHICH IS FILLED WITH LOADS OF BRILLIANT IDEAS TO KEEP YOU BUSY!

SIMPLY COLLECT RUBBISH FROM AROUND THE HOUSE, PICK A PROJECT, ROLL UP YOUR SLEEVES AND GET STUCK IN!

YOU DON'T HAVE TO BE GOOD AT ART, JUST CRAZY ABOUT IT!

WHAT'S INSIDE!

DIPPY DINOSAUR!

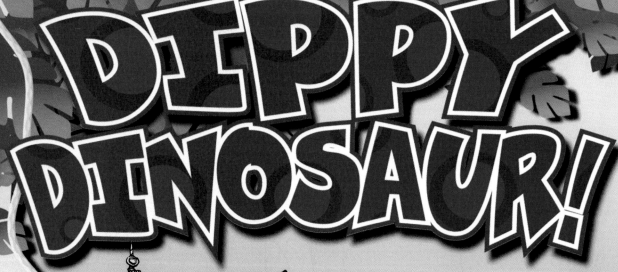

1 Cover a blown-up balloon with six layers of papier maché and leave it to dry overnight. Burst the balloon and you have the body.

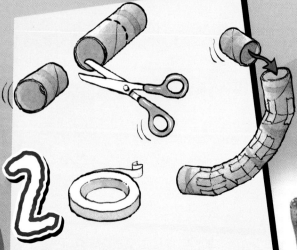

2 Make the curved neck by cutting toilet roll tubes into 4cm or 5cm lengths and joining them together with sticky tape.

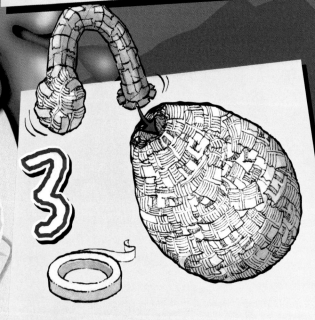

3 For the head, crumple a sheet of newspaper and tape it to one end of the neck. Cut little slits in the opposite end of the neck and fold these back to form tabs. Tape it to the body.

4 Cut a slit in the head to form a mouth and attach a piece of cardboard inside with sticky tape.

5 Make legs by cutting a slit in 4 cardboard tubes, then curl the tubes and tape them into cone shapes. Cut little slits in the larger end of each cone to make tabs, and tape these to the body.

6 For the tail, roll a sheet of newspaper into a long sausage. Curl it round and tape it down well. Attach it to the body with sticky tape.

PVA

7 Now cover the whole thing with two layers of newspaper strips and diluted PVA glue, paying attention to all the joins. Leave to dry until hard.

8 Finally paint your dinosaur with poster paint. You can paint him any colour you choose! When he is dry, you can clip notes to the holder in his mouth!

HIDDEN COLOURS!

Find the colours in the grid below. The words can be written vertically, horizontally, diagonally and even backwards!

R	J	B	L	A	C	K	W	E	G
F	T	T	Z	S	T	R	V	D	R
P	U	R	P	L	E	U	Q	A	E
I	R	W	U	E	A	C	K	L	E
N	Q	E	L	M	A	R	O	O	N
K	U	O	D	P	U	C	E	T	F
R	O	R	A	N	G	E	G	L	W
N	I	T	Y	E	L	R	I	V	H
W	S	R	U	J	D	A	E	T	I
Y	E	L	L	O	W	K	B	Y	T
F	B	R	O	W	N	N	L	X	E

YELLOW

BLUE   TURQUOISE

RED   BROWN   BLACK   GREY   PURPLE

PINK   PUCE

ORANGE   WHITE   MAROON   BEIGE   MAUVE

GREEN

9

Zebra Shelf

BRING SOME ANIMAL MAGIC TO YOUR ROOM WITH THIS STRIPE-TASTIC ZEBRA SHELF!

1

Cut two dividers from the shoe box lid and glue these in place inside the box.

2

From cardboard, cut a basic head shape, then wrap this with several layers of newspaper, to pad out the shape.

YOU WILL NEED:

Shoebox and lid, 4 cardboard tubes, card, sticky tape, newspaper, PVA glue, black and white tissue paper, string, paints.

3

Cover the box and the head with about four layers of papier maché. Leave to dry. Then glue the head to one corner of the box. Leave until the glue is dry.

4

Make holes in the base of the box, and in one end of each cardboard tube, and attach the legs to the 'body'.

5

Now have fun decorating your zebra shelf. Paint it white all over - you may need two coats - then paint black stripes.

6

Make the tail by plaiting one sheet of black tissue paper and two sheets of white. Roll each sheet lengthways into a long sausage, flatten, then staple the three sheets together at one end. Plait, then bind the end with string and attach the tail to the box.

FLYING HIGH!

WHAT TO DO:

1 Photocopy the opposite page as many times as you wish or trace it onto plain paper.

2 Then stick it onto thick card to make the picture strong.

3 Decorate it however you want to. I've cut shiny, colourful sweet wrappers into small squares and stuck them on to make a bright, mosaic balloon.

4 As for the rest of the picture, I just coloured it in with felt tips.

CAN YOU THINK OF OTHER WAYS TO DECORATE YOUR BALLOON?

What about making a collage from ripped up magazines or other materials?

You could draw an intricate pattern on the balloon and colour it in using dots, stripes or shapes.

How about using prints? Use sponge or potato to print a colourful pattern!

ART ATTACK

14

TRACE IT!

Can you face a laugh? Simply trace the pictures from the left onto the right hand panel to create some hilarious cartoon faces!

HIGHLY STRUNG

USE STRING, TWINE OR THICK THREAD TO CREATE SOME HIGHLY ORIGINAL PRINTS!

string prints

1) Wrap a long piece of string around an old rolling pin or bottle, fastening it tightly with sticky tape.

2) Spread acrylic paint or printing ink over a plastic sheet. Then roll the rolling pin over, so the string is coated with paint.

3) Roll the rolling pin over a sheet of tissue paper. Do this in more than one direction, so the lines cross and make an interesting pattern. Leave it to dry.

GLUE THE TISSUE PAPER TO A PIECE OF CARD, TO MAKE A GREETINGS CARD.

USE THE PRINTED PAPER TO WRAP A GIFT AND MAKE A MATCHING GIFT TAG.

COVER A SCHOOL BOOK.

18

String blocks

A simple pattern, repeated all over a piece of paper, is called a repeat pattern! It's how a lot of wallpapers and fabrics are printed. Make your own design with cardboard and string and repeat it to make patterned paper that could be used as wrapping paper, a book covering or anything you wish!

You will need:

thick cardboard box card,
acrylic paints or printing inks,
sheet of plastic,
coloured paper,
string,
PVA glue,
roller.

1) Cut the cardboard into squares. These can be any size, but 3cm or 4cm is easy to handle.

2) Dip pieces of string in PVA glue and stick on to card squares, creating simple shapes. Leave to dry thoroughly.

3) Roll out some printing ink or paint on a sheet of plastic, then roll the ink on to the printing block you've made, so the string is well coated.

4) Press the block on to paper and lift off, to make a print. Repeat until you have covered the paper. Leave to dry.

Top Tips!

Keep your pattern simple. The simplest designs are often the most effective. Instead of repeating the same pattern all over the paper, why not combine two or more designs?

DIARY

HOW TO D

HERE'S THE PURR-FECT WAY TO LEARN HOW TO DRAW CATS. FOLLOW THE EASY STEPS, HAVE A PRACTICE, THEN TRY ONE OF YOUR OWN OVER THE PAGE.

This cute kitty has a round head and peanut shaped body. Add legs and erase unwanted lines. Then draw the details on the head.

Copy this cat if you want to draw a cat on the move. Again start with simple round and oval shapes. A triangle shape helps you to draw the back leg. As the cat is running the front legs curve in towards the body. Rub out unwanted lines before you colour him in.

PAW....CATS!

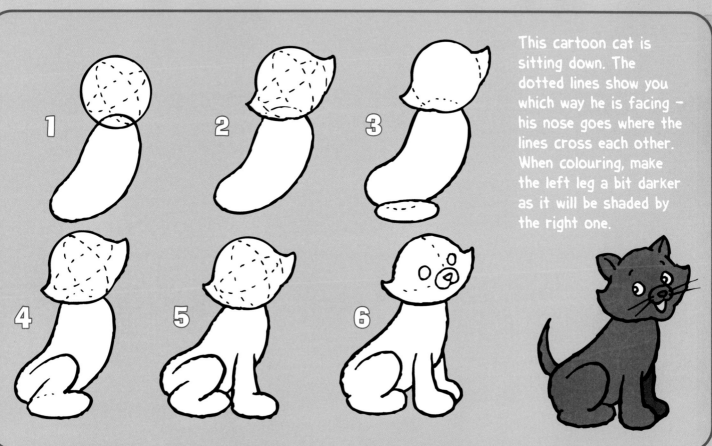

This cartoon cat is sitting down. The dotted lines show you which way he is facing – his nose goes where the lines cross each other. When colouring, make the left leg a bit darker as it will be shaded by the right one.

How about drawing this cuddly, fat cat? He's balancing on a fence. His body is a large oval and the head is small and round. Add some more detail to his coat if you want to make it a tabby cat.

HINTS AND TIPS!

EVERYONE CAN LEARN TO DRAW, THERE'S NO SUCH THING AS 'CAN'T!' YOU DON'T NEED MUCH; SOME PAPER, PENCILS AND A RUBBER, AND YOU'RE AWAY! BELOW YOU'LL FIND SOME SUGGESTIONS TO HELP YOU DEVELOP THOSE DRAWING SKILLS.

COMPOSITION!

When you are thinking about drawing a picture it's good to consider the 'composition' or the layout of the picture. You need to plan where the focal point will be, what will be in the background and how to use the space. To help you, use a 'viewfinder' made from card or paper. Make a simple frame like this one and hold it up to find the composition you are happy to draw.

BE SQUARE!

Another way to improve your drawing skills and help you with harder pictures is to use a grid. If you want to draw from pictures or photos draw a grid of squares on some tracing paper and place it over the picture. Draw another grid on some plain paper. (They must have the same number of squares) Now copy the picture, square by square.

GOING DOTTY!

Rather than using lines to draw, try something different. Colour a picture entirely with dots! Start with an outline, then go on to fill in the whole thing with different coloured dots. In fact, if you take a close look at a newspaper, you'll see that the pictures are made up from hundreds of tiny dots.

CREATIVE KIT!

You don't even have to use pencils to draw! Use lots of different materials to draw with; experiment using felt pens, chalk, crayons, ink pen, ball point pen, anything!

BLAST OFF!

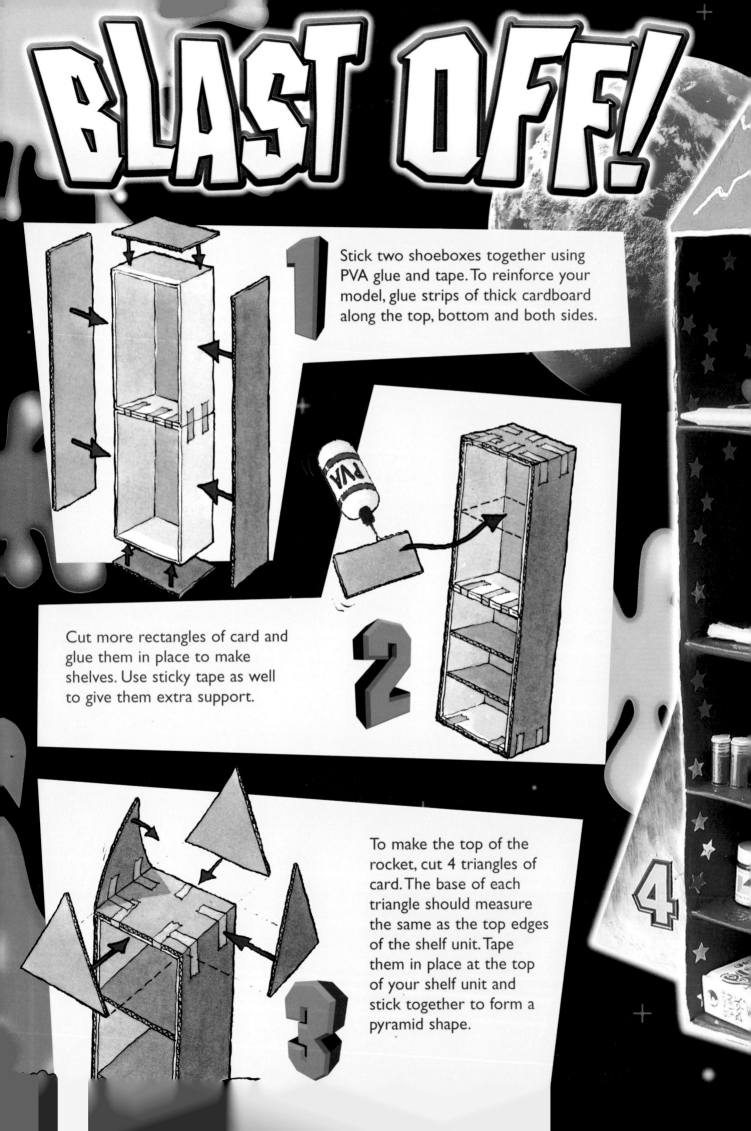

1 Stick two shoeboxes together using PVA glue and tape. To reinforce your model, glue strips of thick cardboard along the top, bottom and both sides.

Cut more rectangles of card and glue them in place to make shelves. Use sticky tape as well to give them extra support. **2**

To make the top of the rocket, cut 4 triangles of card. The base of each triangle should measure the same as the top edges of the shelf unit. Tape them in place at the top of your shelf unit and stick together to form a pyramid shape. **3**

4

YOU WILL NEED:
Cardboard box card, 2 shoeboxes, sticky tape, newspaper, PVA glue, paints.

4 Cut 2 triangular fins from cardboard and stick to the sides of the unit. Then cover the structure with three layers of newspaper strips and diluted PVA glue. Pay particular attention to all the joins. Leave it to dry overnight.

5 Paint the shelves any colours you like. You can add flames coming from the bottom or stick stars all over it. I even drew astronauts and stuck them on the sides.

USE YOUR SHELVES FOR BOOKS, CDS, ART STUFF OR TOYS. MY SHELF IS GOING TO BE REALLY USEFUL IN THE STUDIO!

NEED AN OUTFIT FOR A FANCY DRESS PARTY, A PLAY OR FEEL LIKE TROTTING AROUND THE LIVING ROOM? TRY THIS...

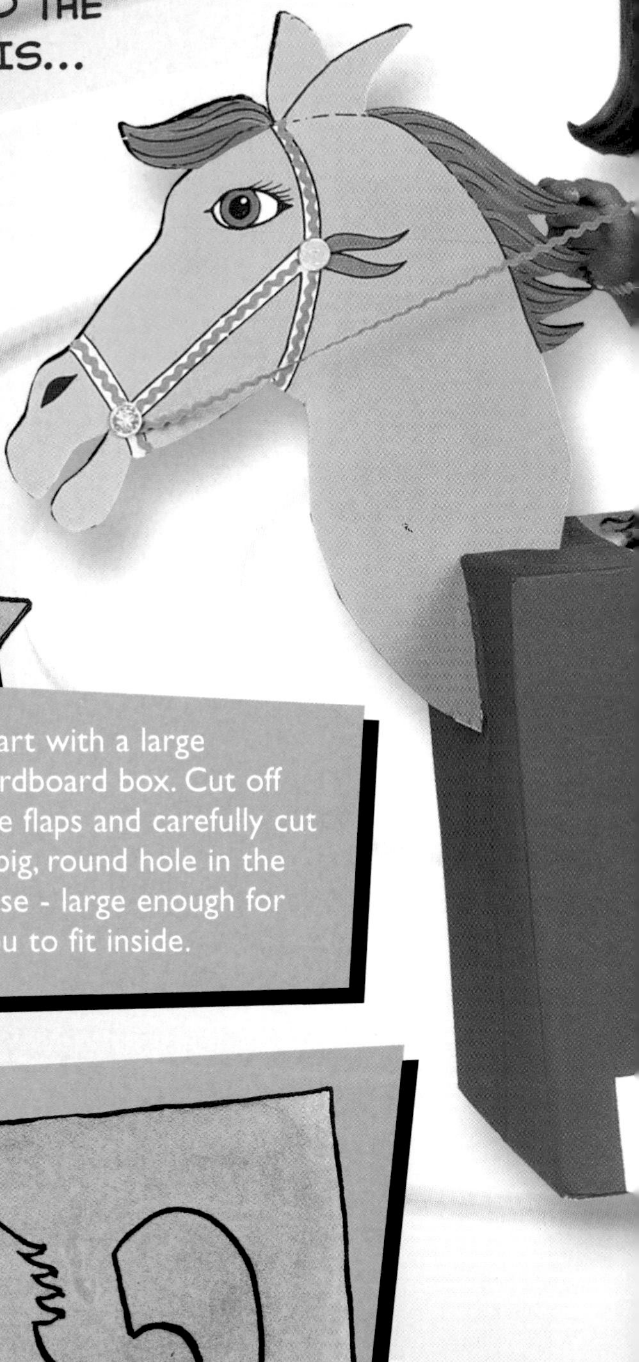

1

Start with a large cardboard box. Cut off the flaps and carefully cut a big, round hole in the base - large enough for you to fit inside.

2

Draw a horse's head and tail on cardboard box card. Make them large enough to be in proportion to the box. Cut these out.

YOU WILL NEED:
Large cardboard box and card, scissors, pencil, paints, ribbon or string, 4 buttons or chocolate coins.

3

Draw two legs on cardboard, one for each side of the box. (They need to be longer than the height of the box.) Cut them out.

4

Now carefully cut 2 slits in the box - front and back - for the head and tail to slot into.

Paint all the pieces. You will need to draw a saddle on the box and give the horse's face plenty of character. Paint trousers on the legs and then stick them to each side of the box.

Now make 2 holes either side of the hole in the body. Tie a length of string through each side to make carrying straps for your shoulders.

Glue card, braid or string on the horse's head to make a bridle. Add buttons or chocolate coins to make the bridle's brass buttons. Finally add some extra string to make some reins. Giddyup

CHALK ATTACK!

Use different coloured chalks and black paper to get creative!
Have a look at these ideas and then make a few pictures of your own.

Use the chalks to draw a sharp outline on some black paper, then cut it out and stick it on to white paper.

Alternatively, make the outline softer and use a whole piece of black paper for your picture.

Use coloured chalks to draw a picture and colour it in. Be careful as this can get a bit messy and you want to avoid smudging the colours.

Then again, smudging can be very effective! Take a look at the effect caused by drawing some yellow dots and using your finger to smudge them - you can create bright stars!

ZARD SCHOOL

Metamorphosis

a) child to frog

b) child to spider

c) slug

Wiz stinx

Paul Gamble

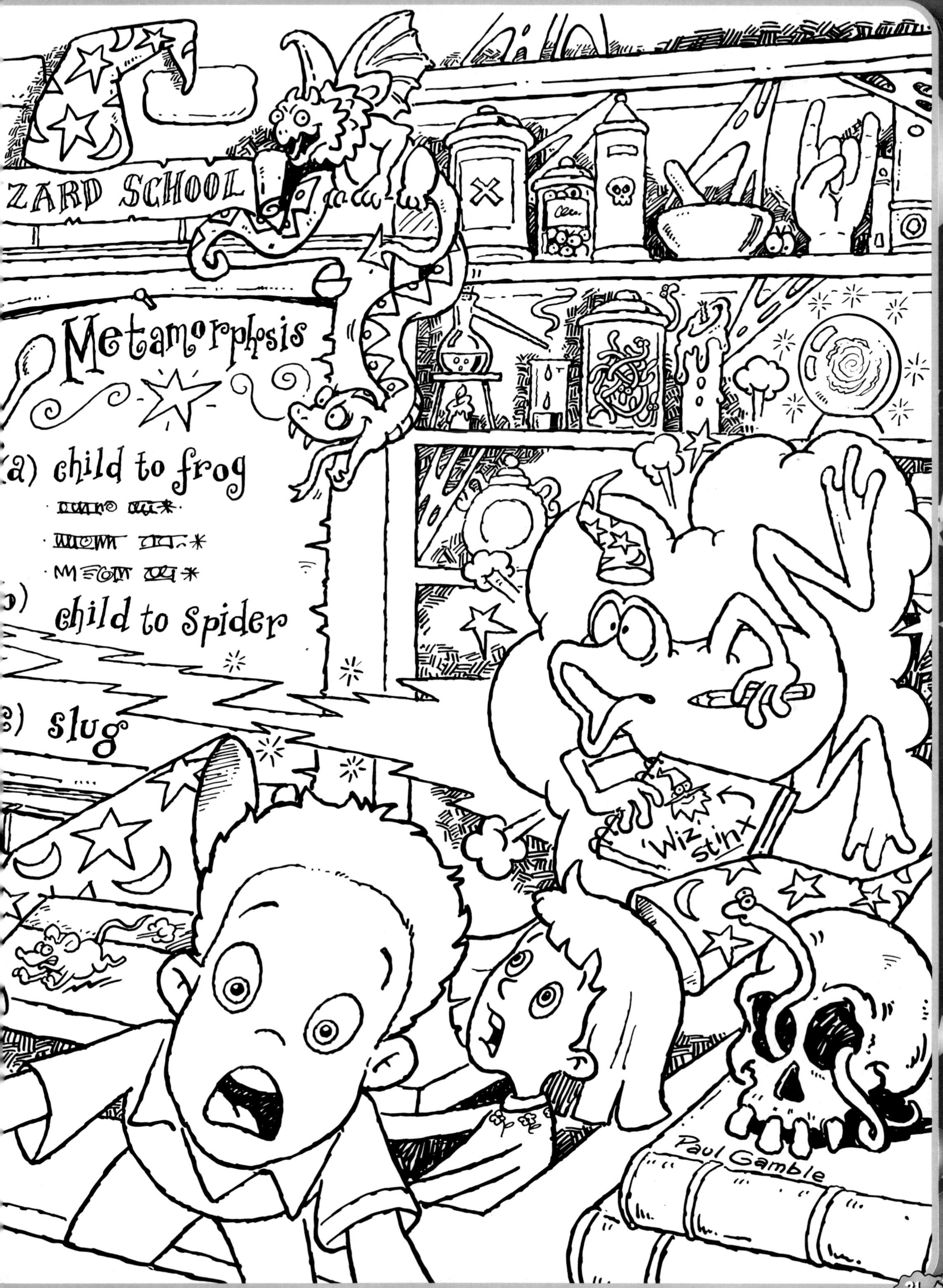

Feline Face!

1 Start with a box about 19cm x 29cm x 6cm (a cereal box, for example). Measure 6cm from each of the bottom corners and cut them off along this line.

2 Stick the corners to the top of the box using plenty of sticky tape to make them really secure. Cut away the back of the box.

3 Cut rectangles from the back piece to fit across the bottom two corners and the open sides of the ears like this. Stick in place.

4 Carefully cut out a nose shaped flap in the front. Cut small pieces of card to fit along the sides and base of the nose. Tape in place.

HERE'S THE PURR-FECT FANCY DRESS MASK!

YOU WILL NEED:
Cereal box, newspaper, PVA glue, elastic or string, paints.

5 Cut holes for eyes then cover the whole mask with at least three layers of torn newspaper and diluted PVA glue. Leave it to dry until it's rock hard.

6 Paint your mask - you can paint a tabby or black and white cat, or even a tiger's face. Then make two small holes either side. Finally add string or elastic to tie the mask around your head.

GO FISHING!

Have an aqua-atta with these fun fishes! Use whateve you have to decorate them an make them dazzle.

YOU WILL NEED

Tracing paper, pencil, card, scissors, paint, PVA glue, glitter, foil, sweet wrappers.

1 Trace and transfer the fish on the opposite page onto card. (You can photocopy them if you want lots.)

2 Cut your fish out. Make sure you have covered all work surfaces before you start to decorate.

3 You can decorate the fish in any way you want. Use paints, glitter, foil, sequins, sweet wrappers – anything!

34

SWISS CHALET

1 Cut down a box as shown in this picture or construct one from card.

2 Make the roof from two pieces of card - make sure that they are large enough to overlap the edges of the box. Tape them securely to the top.

3 Make a balcony. Cut out two strips of card about 1cm wide and lay them flat. Glue small strips in between to form slats.

4 Make the sides and bottom of the balcony from card and then stick the whole thing to the front of the box.

36

YOU WILL NEED:

Cardboard box, card, PVA glue, sticky tape, newspaper, PVA glue, paints.

5

Take another piece of card and fold it into a concertina shape to make the steps. Tape two triangular sides onto the steps and secure to the front of your chalet with sticky tape.

6 Create pretty carved edging by cutting thick card 1cm wide and punching holes all along the edges. Stick this all the way round the roof and along the top.

1cm

7 Cut out small rectangles of card and stick them all round the chalet to form shutters.

8 Cover the whole model with two layers of papier maché. Scrunch up balls of paper soaked in the PVA mixture and stick them around the bottom to make snow. Leave it to dry.

PVA

9 Decorate the whole chalet. Paint it as shown, adding a door, windows and a brick effect on the roof. You could even add a flowery decoration to the front of the balcony.

HINTS AND TIPS!

CHOOSING COLOURS!

When buying watercolours, you will not need white, just your choice of blue, red and yellow.

For poster paints and acrylics, in addition to black and white, try Process Cyan, Process Magenta and Process Yellow, or Cobalt Blue, Poster Red and Lemon.

If you start with a limited palette, you can mix colours together.

COLOUR MIXING!

These squares of colour show what happens when you mix acrylic paints. Try mixing blue with yellow and yellow with magenta, and also see what happens when you mix each of the colours with white...

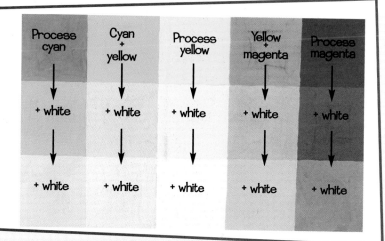

Process cyan	Cyan + yellow	Process yellow	Yellow + magenta	Process magenta
↓	↓	↓	↓	↓
+ white	+ white	+ white	+ white	+ white
↓	↓	↓	↓	↓
+ white	+ white	+ white	+ white	+ white

PRIMARIES & SECONDARIES!

The three primary colours are red, blue and yellow. Can you answer these colour mixing questions?

What do you get if you mix...
...Red and blue? Blue and yellow? Yellow and red?

The answers are purple, green and orange, the secondary colours.

HERE ARE THE PRIMARY AND SECONDARY COLOURS, PAINTED IN ACRYLIC PAINTS ON A PEBBLE, TO MAKE A RAINBOW!

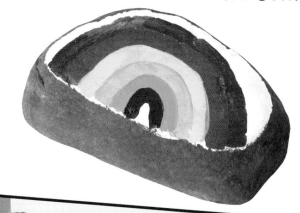

EXPERIMENT WITH COLOUR MIXING! BUT DON'T STICK TO PAPER - CHECK OUT THIS COLOURFUL PLANT POT!

Trap-easy!

1 Wash and dry two plastic bottles - washing up liquid ones are best. Carefully cut them in half and remove the lids. (Ask an adult to help you with this.) Crumple two pieces of newspaper into balls for the heads and tape to the bottle necks.

2 For the girl, tape a plastic bowl or large yogurt pot to the bottom of the cut off bottle, for a skirt. For the male trapeze artist, squeeze the bottle together at the bottom and tape shut with lots of sticky tape.

3 For the arms and legs you can use rolled up corrugated card. Roll it up tightly and tape down. Then tape them onto the bottle. Remember they will be swinging from a trapeze so fix the arms upwards. Bend the legs of the male artist so he can hang over his trapeze.

SWING INTO ACTION WITH THIS TRAP-EASY ART ATTACK! FOLLOW THE STEPS TO BRING THE BIG TOP TO YOUR BEDROOM...

YOU WILL NEED!

Plastic bottles, newspaper, cardboard, string, yogurt pot, sticky tape, PVA glue, paints.

4

For the trapeze, put string onto a rectangle of cardboard leaving the ends coming out of each side, roll up tightly and tape down with sticky tape. Cut the string to the length you want and knot together. Make another one if you want a trapeze for each doll.

5

Mix two parts PVA glue with one part water. Dip pieces of torn newspaper into the mixture and stick to the models. Cover the models with three layers of paper. Shape the faces using tissue soaked in PVA glue and water. Leave to dry until they are rock hard.

PVA

6

When the models have dried, paint the trapeze artists with bright colours. Paint the trapeze and let that dry too. Finally glue the trapeze artists to the trapezes. What about making another one and attaching it to the hands or feet of the other ones?

PVA

AIR HEADS!

THESE BRILLIANT BALLOON HEADS
ARE SUCH FUN AND SO EASY TO MAKE –
THEY'LL BLOW YOU AWAY!

WHAT TO DO:

Blow up round balloons and knot them. Secure
them to a decorated cardboard sticky tape reel
or a cylinder of corrugated card with sticky tape.
This forms a neck and helps them stand up.

Now create a balloon head! Cut out ears, noses,
mouths, hair, eyelashes and cheeks from coloured
card and glue onto the balloon.

USE YOUR IMAGINATION TO CREATE LOTS
OF WEIRD AND WACKY CHARACTERS!

43

BIG HEAD!

THIS IS THE ONE TIME IT'S GREAT TO HAVE A BIG HEAD!
THESE GREAT CARNIVAL HEADS ARE A REAL LAUGH AND
GREAT FUN TO MAKE AND WEAR!

1 Cut seven leaf shaped segments from corrugated card with the ridges running across the segments. (Each segment needs to be about 56cm long and 18cm wide.)

56cm

18cm

2 Join the segments together using sticky tape starting at the top. Join two pieces then add a third and so on. Leave the bottom open bending the segments back slightly.

3 Cut a strip of corrugated card about 12cm wide and long enough to go all the way round to form a collar. Stick this on the bottom and tape each segment to the inside. Make sure it is big enough to put your head through.

44

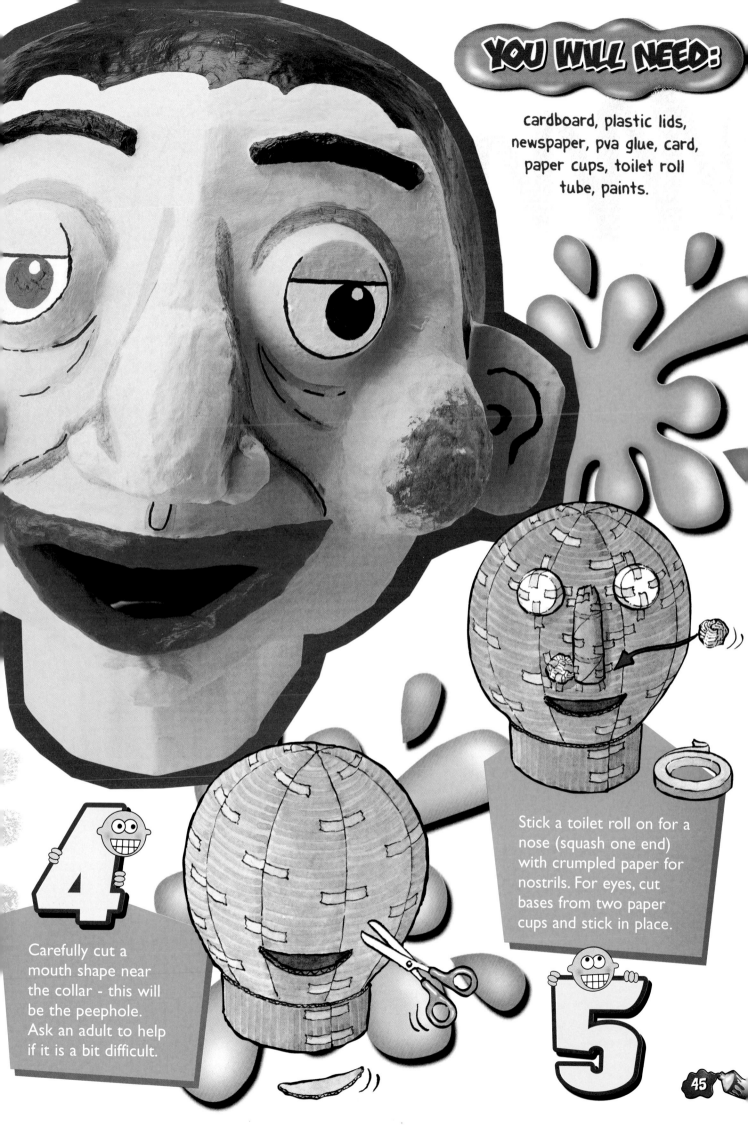

cardboard, plastic lids, newspaper, pva glue, card, paper cups, toilet roll tube, paints.

Stick a toilet roll on for a nose (squash one end) with crumpled paper for nostrils. For eyes, cut bases from two paper cups and stick in place.

4

Carefully cut a mouth shape near the collar - this will be the peephole. Ask an adult to help if it is a bit difficult.

5

45

6 Roll up thin sausages of newspaper and tape in place for lips and eyebrows. Cut out cardboard ears and tape in place on the sides.

7 Cover the head with five layers of torn newspaper and diluted PVA glue, paying attention to the joins. Papier maché inside the collar too. For tricky areas like the nose use strips of kitchen paper.

PVA

8 Leave the head until it is completely dry. Now you can paint it with bright colours. Make it look as crazy as you dare!

PAINT IT ANY COLOUR YOU LIKE! I MADE ANOTHER ONE LOOK REALLY GHOULISH BY PAINTING IT GREEN AND RED.

PENGUIN POP-OUT!

1 Photocopy the picture onto white paper and stick it onto thin card. Cut it out.

2 Fold it in half along the vertical dotted line.

3 Carefully cut the small red dotted line and fold the other dotted lines to push the beak outwards.

4 Finally, write a message on the back!

SUPER SUNDAE

UNFORTUNATELY YOU CAN'T EAT THIS DELICIOUS LOOKING ICE CREAM BUT YOU CAN USE IT TO STORE YOUR PENS AND PENCILS...

1 Curl a piece of thin card or thick paper into a cone. Trim the top, so it's the same diameter or slightly smaller than a cheesebox.

2 Snip the pointed end of the cone and tape it to one half of the cheesebox.

3 For the 'lid,' stick a large yogurt pot or round margarine tub to the other half of the cheesebox. Cut a wafer shape from card and stick in place. Tape two cut down drinking straws to the lid too.

YOU WILL NEED:
Thin card, sticky tape, scissors, cheese box,
large yogurt pot or round margarine tub, 2 drinking straws,
newspaper, PVA glue, paints.

4

Add some crumpled kitchen paper and a round ball of crumpled newspaper to the margarine tub to make a cherry.

5

Cover the base and lid with at least four layers of diluted PVA glue and torn newspaper strips. Leave it to dry until rock hard.

PVA

6

Have fun painting your sundae! For the sauce, dilute red paint until it's quite runny and pour over the top so that it drips down. Paint fruit shapes on the cone.

TRY MAKING DIFFERENT SHAPED ICE CREAM SUNDAES WITH DIFFERENT COLOURS TO SHOW OTHER FLAVOURS.

Get Sorted

1

Arrange your tubes on a piece of cardboard box card in the shape of a socks or pants. When you're happy with the arrangement, glue the tubes to the card and each other.

2

Leave the glue to dry, then trim around the shape. Cut a long strip of card, the same width as the loo roll tubes and wrap it right round, taping it to the tubes as you go.

3

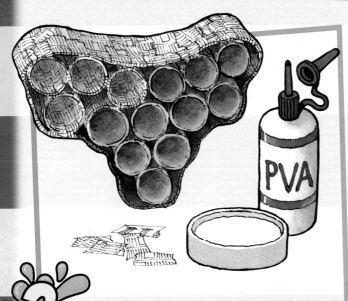

Now cover the whole construction with about three layers of papier maché. Leave to dry until it's rock hard.

4

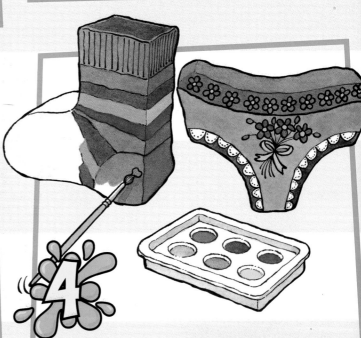

Paint your models white all over, then paint colourful stripes on the sock and a pretty pattern on the pants. Or paint the pants to look like sporty Y-fronts! It's up to you!

YOU WILL NEED:
Cardboard box card,
toilet rolls,
sticky tape,
newspaper,
PVA glue,
paints.

SCREEN SHOT!

DRAW A CLIP, IMAGE OR CHARACTER FROM ONE OF YOUR FAVOURITE MOVIES!

PERFECT PUPPETS!

PUT ON YOUR OWN
PUNCH AND JUDY SHOW WITH
THIS MINI PUPPET SET!

YOU WILL NEED:

Scissors, felt tip pens
or coloured pencils,
glue, large empty
matchbox, dead
matchsticks.

1 You will find all the pictures you need on pages 54 and 55. These pages can be photocopied so you don't ruin your annual.

2 Colour all the pictures in including all the little characters and the scenery.

3 Carefully cut everything out. Remember to cut the window out in the theatre section. Also cut a square away from one end of the matchbox after you have removed the tray.

4 Now fold along the dotted lines on the theatre piece and wrap it around the matchbox making sure the window hole rests over the hole in the matchbox. Stick down.

5 Now fold along the dotted lines and wrap each puppet around one end of a long DEAD matchstick and glue together.

6 You should be able to place a background picture in the tray and slip it back into the matchbox so that the scenery shows through. You can change these pictures as you tell your story.

"That's the way to do it"

CUT OUT

Punch
~ and ~
Judy

THAT'S
THE WAY TO
DO IT!

Boink!

Try making your own puppet theatre using a matchbox. You can decorate it how you like, make different scenery and characters. You can tell all sorts of stories or make up one of your own. Use your imagination!

55

NATIVE ART

THE DESIRE TO DRAW AND PAINT, OFTEN TO TELL STORIES, HAS BEEN AROUND FOR THOUSANDS OF YEARS - BEFORE PAPER EVER EXISTED! THE ARTISTS WOULD USE BARK OR STONE TO EXPRESS THEMSELVES. I'VE USED SAND PAPER TO CREATE SOME ANCIENT ART...

ALL YOU NEED IS SOME SANDPAPER, AN OLD PAINTBRUSH AND SOME PAINTS!

WHAT TO DO:

1 Use a pencil to sketch out your drawing on the rough side of the sandpaper. Make it very simple.

2 Mix up some 'earthy' coloure paint. These would be browns oranges and black. You can u red or green too as fruit wa often used to make colours.

3 Dab paint onto your sandpap picture. Can you see I've use white to highlight the edges?

SO TRY IT YOURSELF - CREATE SOME NATIVE ART...

Panorama Picture!

MAKE A PICTURE WITH A DIFFERENCE! USE SEVERAL LAYERS TO CREATE A 3 DIMENSIONAL SCENE.

WHAT TO DO:

1 You'll find all the pictures over the page. Photocopy the pages if you don't want to ruin your annual. Cut out and colour in all the pictures.

2 You will need 2 pieces of thin card measuring 380mm x 85mm. Fold them in a concertina style with folds 25mm wide.

3 In order, so you have picture number 1 at the front and picture number 8 at the back, start sticking the pictures into the folds of one of the concertina pieces. After you have done one side, stick on the other concertina piece of card.

4 When you look through the front hole you should be able to see all the way to the back picture. You should be able to fold the picture flat or pull it out so that a corridor is formed along the middle.

COPY THIS IDEA TO HAVE A GO AT MAKING YOUR OWN PANORAMA PICTURES. JUST MIND YOUR FINGERS IF YOU'RE CUTTING OUT SMALL AREAS WITH SCISSORS.

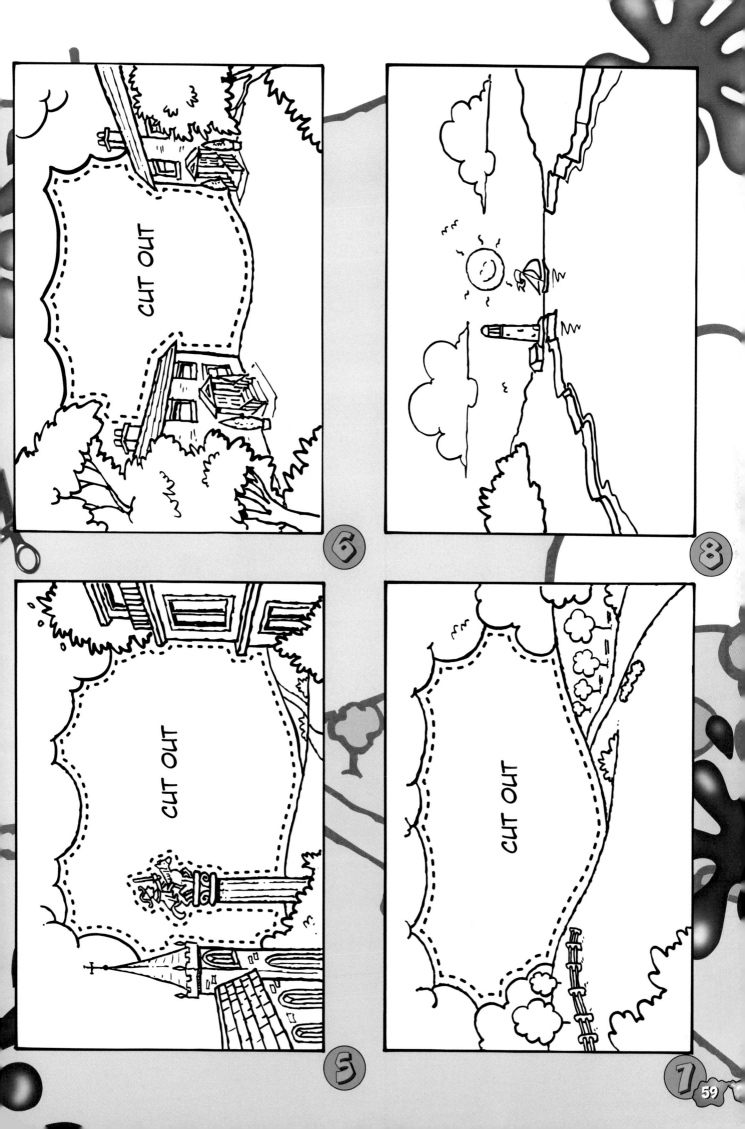

CUT OUT

CUT OUT

CUT OUT

6

8

5

7

BE QUICK OFF THE DRAW WITH THESE TIPS ON CREATING COWBOYS. CREATE YOUR OWN CARTOON WESTERN AND DRIVE THE BADDY OUT OF TOWN!

1 Start with a peanut shaped body, an oval head and the left leg.

2 Add the right leg in the foreground.

3 Now add the arms - the left one is raised - with round circles for hands. Draw a waistband.

4 Add pointy feet shapes and draw a waistcoat and sheriff's badge.

5 Draw bows on the trousers and create sleeves. Erase any unwanted pencil lines.

6 Add details such as a scarf, and a gun and holster. Draw fingers on each hand like this.

Follow these 4 steps to draw your cowboy's head and face.

Pop!

Finally draw a fun gun in his left hand, add some spurs and colour!

1

This one is a baddy. Give him a huge body and draw the head low down so he'll look mean.

2

Draw 2 sausage shaped legs imaging that the knees face your left. Draw a waistband.

3

Add pointy feet and lines to show boots. Erase pencils lines where you see dotted lines.

4

Draw large, powerful arms with circles for hands. Add a scarf and a gun belt.

5

Add fingers to the round hands and erase unwanted pencil lines.

1

2

3

Follow these 3 steps to draw your baddy's head and face.

Finally, colour the baddy!

TRY IT YOURSELF!

USE THE TIPS YOU'VE LEARNED TO CREATE A SHOWDOWN BETWEEN THE SHERIFF AND THE BAD GUY...

FANTASY PHONE!

EVER WANTED TO DESIGN YOUR OWN MOBILE PHONE COVER? USE THE TEMPLATES BELOW TO HAVE A GO AND THEN ADD A TEXT MESSAGE...

HOW ABOUT DESIGNING ONE FOR DAYTIME AND ONE FOR NIGHT TIME?

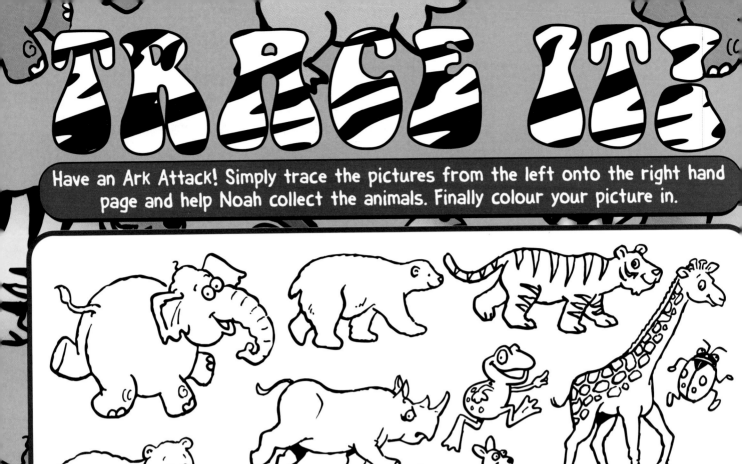

TRACE IT!

Have an Ark Attack! Simply trace the pictures from the left onto the right hand page and help Noah collect the animals. Finally colour your picture in.

BEACH BOOK

THE SUMMER HOLIDAYS ARE HERE AT LAST.
GET IN THE MOOD FOR RELAXATION AND FUN WITH
THESE BRILLIANT BEACH BOOKENDS.

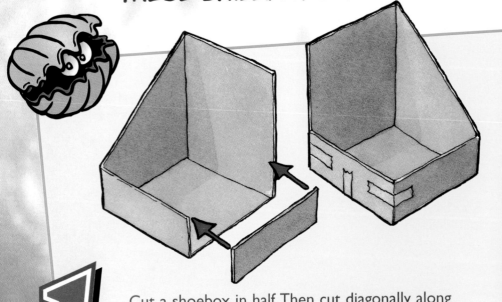

1 Cut a shoebox in half. Then cut diagonally along the ends and cut away one side of each, leaving two small sections like this. Stick two small rectangles of card along the open sides.

2 Cut a boat shape from cardboard - cut a second shape the same and stick it to the first bit to make it thicker. Stick this to the base of one of the sections.

3 On the other section stick the base cut from a plastic cup. Glue a pencil or stick in the cup to create the handle of the umbrella. Glue another stick or pencil behind the boat shape to make a mast.

4

Roll up small balls of newspaper and glue them to the sides of the plastic cup to build up a mound.

5

To make the top of the umbrella, cut the rim off a paper plate. Cut a slit in the plate from edge to centre, overlap the slit edges and tape down on the underside to form a shallow cone.

6 Cover everything except the sticks with three layers of torn newspaper and diluted PVA glue. Leave to dry. Then glue the umbrella to the stick in the mound.

7 Paint both bookends. Paint the umbrella side with a blue sky and yellow sand. Paint the boat surrounded by blue sea. Leave them to dry.

8 Brush glue inside the bases and over the mound under the umbrella. Beneath the boat, push some crumpled blue plastic or fabric. Sprinkle sand over the mound and put some small pebbles in the base.

9 Finally, fix some paper sails to the boat's mast with a spot of glue and attach some string from the top of the mast down to each end of the boat.

HiNTS AND TiPS!

A lot of the materials used in collage you will probably already have or at least be able to get hold of very easily! Save scraps of paper and card – as many different kinds as you can – to give as much colour and texture as possible to your projects.

HERE ARE A FEW THINGS YOU CAN COLLECT:

coloured paper
envelopes
magazines
comics
cardboard box card
sweet wrappers
lolly sticks
wrapping paper
string

HERE ARE A FEW THINGS YOU MAY HAVE TO BUY:

glue stick
PVA glue
glitter glue
sticky tape
pipe cleaners
goggly eyes
corrugated paper
sequins

THIS PICTURE OF A ROCKET SHOWS HOW YOU CAN ACHIEVE TEXTURED EFFECTS QUITE SIMPLY.

The body of the rocket is cut from some fancy silver corrugated card and the fins from other shiny card. The nose cone and booster are coloured foil from chocolates. The big gold star is cut from gold corrugated card and the other stars are the gummed ones you can buy in packets from stationers. The lettering is cut from sparkly self-adhesive book covering paper.

69

SOCK PUPPET

LOST A SOCK IN THE WASH? WELL HERE'S A GREAT WAY TO MAKE USE OF THE OTHER ONE! MAKE IT INTO A CUTE AND CUDDLY PUPPET!

1 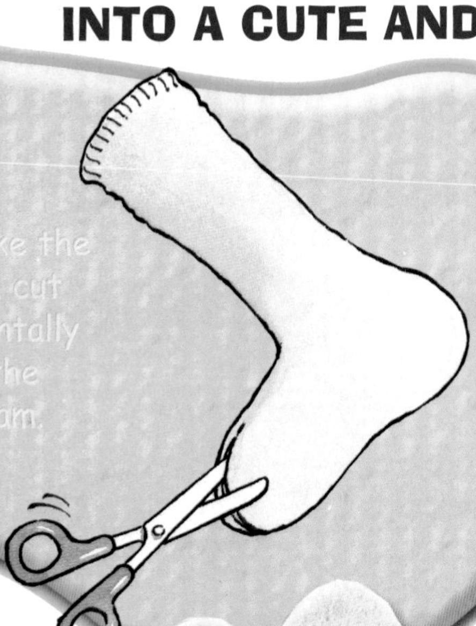 To make the mouth, cut horizontally along the toe seam.

You will need:
Old socks, scissors, card, coloured felt, PVA glue, wool, ribbon.

14 cm

7 cm

2 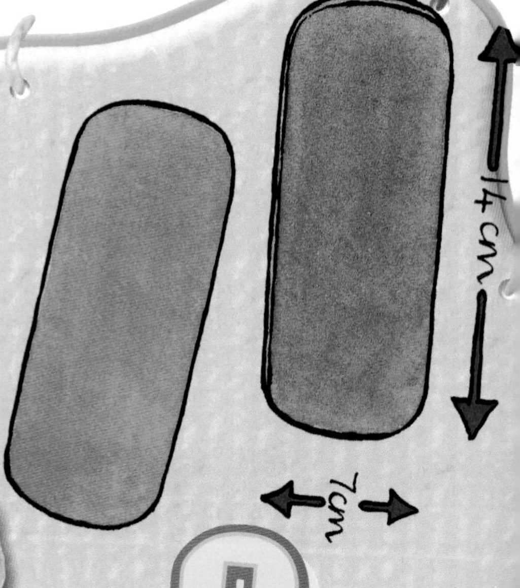 Cut a piece of card about 14cm long and 7cm wide with rounded ends. Draw around this onto pink felt and cut out.

ts!

4

Cut about 15 bunches of wool - about 10cm long. Snip 2 small holes in the back of the puppet. Tie a piece of wool around each bunch, wrap some tape around one end, and push it through the holes. Tie again to fix in place and remove the tape. Do this down the back.

3

Fold the card in half. With your hand inside the sock, position the card in the toe area and stick the edges to the sock. Stick the pink felt on top.

5

Decorate the rest of the sock with ears, eyes and a nose cut from felt stuck on card. For the giraffe, add brown patches and horns and, for the horse add some reins.

JOIN THE CIRCUS!

INSTEAD OF 'THE BIG TOP' MAKE YOUR VERY OWN TINY TOP AND LITTLE CIRCUS PERFORMERS. AND HERE'S HOW...

1 Cut a rectangle of bendy card, bend it into a cylinder shape and tape down. Cut a door shape in one side.

2 Cut a length of bendy card about 4cms wide, bend it round the cylinder shape to measure it and then stick it down. This strip needs to be slightly wider than the cylinder.

4cm

3 Make a lid for the larger cylinder, by curling a paper plate into a cone. Make a base for the strip with a circle of card measured to fit and stick in place.

CIRCU

4 For the caravan, make a curved roof from a rectangle of corrugated card and stick it on top of a small cardboard box. Make wheels by cutting the bases from four polystyrene cups.

5 Cover the models with diluted PVA glue and about three layers of torn newspaper strips. Leave to dry.

CIRCUS

PVA

6 Paint the models, first with white paint, then with bright colours. Yellow and red are traditional circus colours - but you can use any colours that you like!

CIRCUS

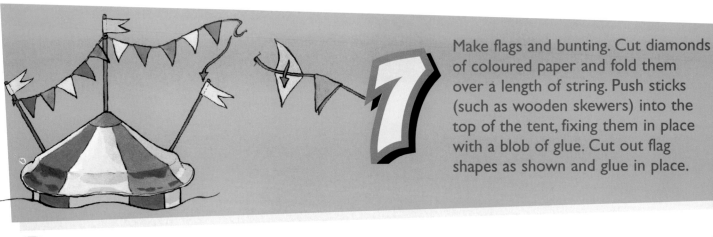

Make flags and bunting. Cut diamonds of coloured paper and fold them over a length of string. Push sticks (such as wooden skewers) into the top of the tent, fixing them in place with a blob of glue. Cut out flag shapes as shown and glue in place.

8 Make circus performers and animals from clay. You can use the coloured modelling clay that you bake in the oven - ask an adult to help - or self-hardening clay which you can paint when it's dry. Keep the figures inside the tent when you are not playing with them.

CIRCUS

WILD IDEAS!

YOU WILL NEED

Thin card, colouring pens,
scissors, 14 paper fasteners.

1 You'll find your bendy animals
over the page. Read these
instructions first if you are
going to cut them out.

2 Cut out or trace off the animals and
stick them onto cereal box card to
make them stronger. If you want to
make lots of them - simply
photocopy the pages.

3 Check which parts
match up and
colour them in.

4 Then attach the pieces with paper
fasteners - you'll need four for the
gorilla and ten for the snake.

GORGEOUS GIRAFFES!

WHAT ABOUT THESE CUT GIRAFFES? STAND THEM ANYWHERE TO CREATE SOME REALLY WILD SHELVES OR JUST TO GIVE YOUR ROOM SOM ANIMAL MAGIC!

1 Tape down the lid of the shoe box, then glue or tape four kitchen roll tubes to the box, one in each corner, to make the giraffe's legs.

2 Either roll up a sheet of corrugated cardboard or use a large cardboard tube for the neck. Tape an empty box on top for the head. Roll up a smaller piece of corrugated card for his tail, then attach a crumpled ball of paper on top.

3 Attach some ears made from cardboard, to the back of the head. Roll up paper or corrugated card for horns, then tape them in place on top of the head. Stick some scrunched up balls of paper on the ends of the horns.

WHAT YOU NEED: small box, shoebox and lid, kitchen roll tubes, corrugated cardboard or large cardboard tube, sticky tape, newspaper, paper, PVA glue, paints.

4

Cover your model with about four layers of papier maché. Then leave the giraffe to dry.

5

When dry, you can draw a pattern of spots all over, large ones on the body and smaller ones on the neck and legs, then get painting!

PVA

YOU CAN CUT A SECTION OUT OF THE BACK TO STORE BITS'N'BOBS IN! WHY NOT MAKE A SMALLER ONE TOO?

Stay in line!

POSTER PAINTS ARE PERFECT FOR CREATING CARTOON LIKE PICTURES AND HERE'S THE SECRET... PAINT IN THE COLOURED AREAS FIRST, THEN GO OVER THE OUTLINES WITH BLACK AFTERWARDS!

Poster paints give a heavier, more solid feel to pictures. The black lines add real emphasis and the pictures stand out.

Mistakes can be easily corrected with poster paints. Once the wrong colour has dried, just overpaint with the colour you want.

If you are using powder paint, mix with a small amount of water at a time. Too much water will make the paint act like watercolour paint.

TOP TIP!

To create the black line, you can use black poster paint or a fine paintbrush - but you will need a very steady hand - you may find it easier to use a black marker pen. Just make sure the paint is completely dry before you add the black lines!

POTS OF FUN!

Try out this eye-catching painting technique by painting a row of pencils. Then cut them out and use them to transform an old coffee tin into a pencil pot.

Try it yourself!

YOU WILL NEED: pencil and ruler, poster paints, coffee or cocoa tin, strip of white paper long enough to go around the tin, strip of black paper long enough to go around the tin, paint brush, black marker pen, glue stick.

1. Using a pencil and ruler, draw a series of parallel lines. These will form the sides of each pencil. Add triangular shapes to the tops of the lines, for the pencil points.

2. Now fill in the pencil shapes with poster paint. Use lots of different colours. Don't forget to add details such as different coloured ends to some of the pencils, or pink erasers!

3. Once the paint is dry, add details using black paint and a fine brush, or a black marker pen.

4. Cover the outside of the tin with black paper. Cut out around the tops of the painted pencils, and stick the painted strip around the tin.

If you need some help drawing a pencil, trace these pencils on to plain paper to use as a template!

WIZARD'S HAT!

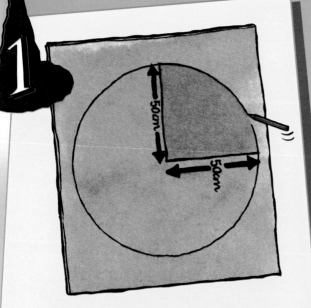

1

Cut out a quarter circle of card with a radius of 50cm. Draw a whole circle first if this helps. Cut out and roll it into a cone shape. Make sure it fits your head before securing with sticky tape.

2

Place the cone onto another piece of card and draw around the base. Then draw another circle a bit bigger to make a ring shape. It doesn't have to be perfect.

3

Cut out the ring. Draw a circle about 2cm inside the inner ring and cut it out. Then carefully snip around the edge to make tabs.

YOU WILL NEED:

Cereal box card, scissors, ruler, sticky tape, pencil, newspaper, PVA glue, paints.

4

Bend the tabs upwards and fit to the cone. Attach with sticky tape.

5

Crumple the hat slightly to give it a bit of character. Cover the whole thing with three layers of torn newspaper pasted on with diluted PVA glue. Pay attention to the joins. Leave to dry.

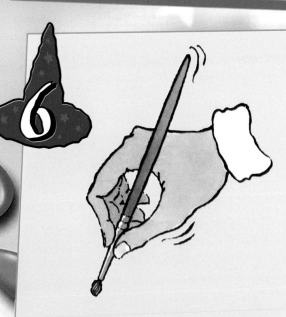

6

When dry, paint. I painted the hat purple and then added some stars in pink. You could decorate it with glitter or sequins to give it a really magical feel.

GAME ON!

HOW ABOUT THIS ANIMAL-TASTIC VERSION OF NOUGHTS AND CROSSES? A BRILLIANT GAME AND MAKE ALL IN ONE.

1 Cut 8 strips of thick card measuring 22cm x 2cm. Layer them on top of each other following the picture as a guide. Tape firmly in place. The central square should be 6cm.

2cm

22cm

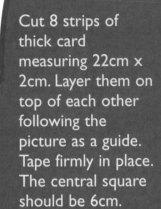

2 Draw ten circles 5cm across on a sheet of thin card. Draw ears on five of them and draw a curved line across the top of the other five. Cut them out.

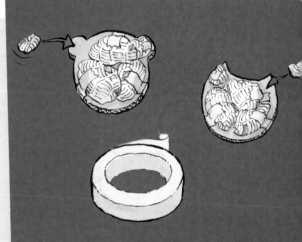

3 Build up the shapes with folded or crumpled pieces of paper, to make the faces more three-dimensional. One will be a monkey, the other a tiger.

4

Cover the cardboard cross and the animal heads with three layers of torn newspaper pasted on with diluted PVA glue. Leave to dry.

5

When dry, paint. The cross could be jungle green, or zebra-striped! Why not paint each side different? Paint five heads like monkeys and the other five like tigers.

85

TRACE IT!

TRACE THE PICTURES BELOW AND THEN TRANSFER THEM ON TO THE RIGHT-HAND PAGE TO CREATE A SUPER SWIMMING SCENE. COLOUR TO COMPLETE THE PICTURE!

FISHY FUN!

TRANSFORM A ROUND BALLOON INTO AN AMAZING FAKE FISH BOWL TO HIDE YOUR SECRET STUFF IN!

1

Start by blowing up a round balloon and knotting it. Tape it to a jam jar and brush all over with diluted PVA glue.

2

Cover the whole balloon - apart from the area inside the jam jar - with torn newspaper strips. Build up at least four layers. Do two layers, leave it to dry then do another two.

3

When it's dry remove it from the jar and pop the balloon. Take the cheesebox, draw around it on the to of the balloon and cut this out to make an opening.

4

Tape one half of the cheesebox to the bottom of the shell to make a base. Place the other half on a piece of card and draw a slightly larger circle around it. Cut this out and stick it to the cheesebox. This will be the lid.

YOU WILL NEED:

Round balloon, cheese box, newspaper, PVA glue, sticky tape, paints.

HOW ABOUT MAKING A FISH FOOD PENCIL POT TO MATCH? USE AN OLD CARDBOARD CONTAINER SUCH AS A TALCUM POWDER TUBE OR MAKE ONE FROM A TOILET ROLL TUBE.

Fish Food

5

Cover the base and the lid with about three layers of papier maché. Cover the cut edge of the opening with strips of paper to make it neat.

6

Leave it to dry, then paint it to look like a fish bowl with fish in it. When finished, the lid should fit snugly inside the opening.

PVA

YOU WILL NEED:

Large piece of card for background, corrugated paper, glue stick, PVA glue, wooden lolly sticks, scraps of fabric, raffia, 2 buttons, 2 goggly eyes, seeds, rice or grain.

CREATE TEXTURE IN YOUR PICTURES USING CORRUGATED PAPER OR CARD. SEE HOW THE RIDGES LOOK A BIT LIKE PLOUGHED FIELDS IN THIS PICTURE.

1) Make the background. Cover the top part of the cardboard with blue paper, for the sky. Cut out fields, hills and trees from corrugated paper - brown, yellow, green and white. Stick them down using a glue stick.

2) Cut out the scarecrow's coat from fabric or paper. Cut out a head, too, and a hat. Glue lolly sticks in place, one vertical and one horizontal to form the scarecrow's body. Glue the other bits of the scarecrow in place, including some bits of raffia for his hair and in his sleeves.

3) Now add all the other details - cut a sack shape from fabric and glue on seeds (these are melon seeds, washed and dried), black paper crows with goggly eyes, trees and a broken fence made from painted lolly sticks.

Top Tips!

You can buy coloured, corrugated paper from craft shops. or save corrugated packaging from boxes and paint it different colours, using poster paints or acrylics, before cutting out your shapes.

A glue stick is ideal for sticking paper, including corrugated paper. For fabric, use a thin layer of PVA. PVA is also ideal for sticking small objects such as buttons, seeds and lolly sticks.

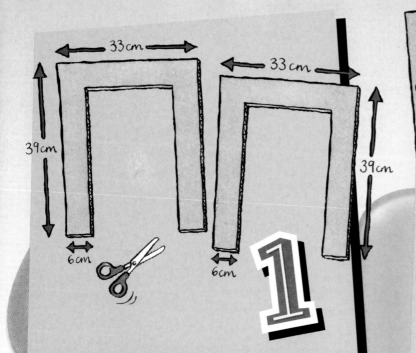

1

Measure and cut out two rectangles of card about 33cm x 39cm. Use thick cardboard cut from a strong cardboard box. Draw a 6cm border around three sides and cut the centre part from both rectangles.

2

Cut slots in the side pieces, halfway up. (Use the picture as a guide.) On one piece the slots should be cut on the inside while on the second piece, the slots should be cut on the outside. Slot the two pieces together.

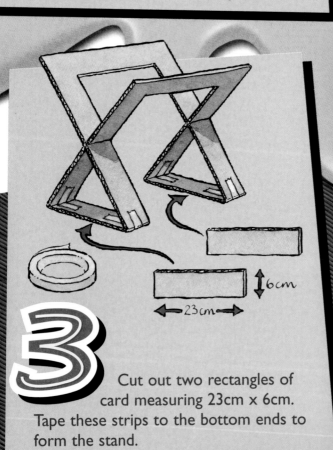

3

Cut out two rectangles of card measuring 23cm x 6cm. Tape these strips to the bottom ends to form the stand.

4

Cover the whole thing with two smooth layers of torn newspaper pasted on with diluted PVA glue. Pay attention to the joins.

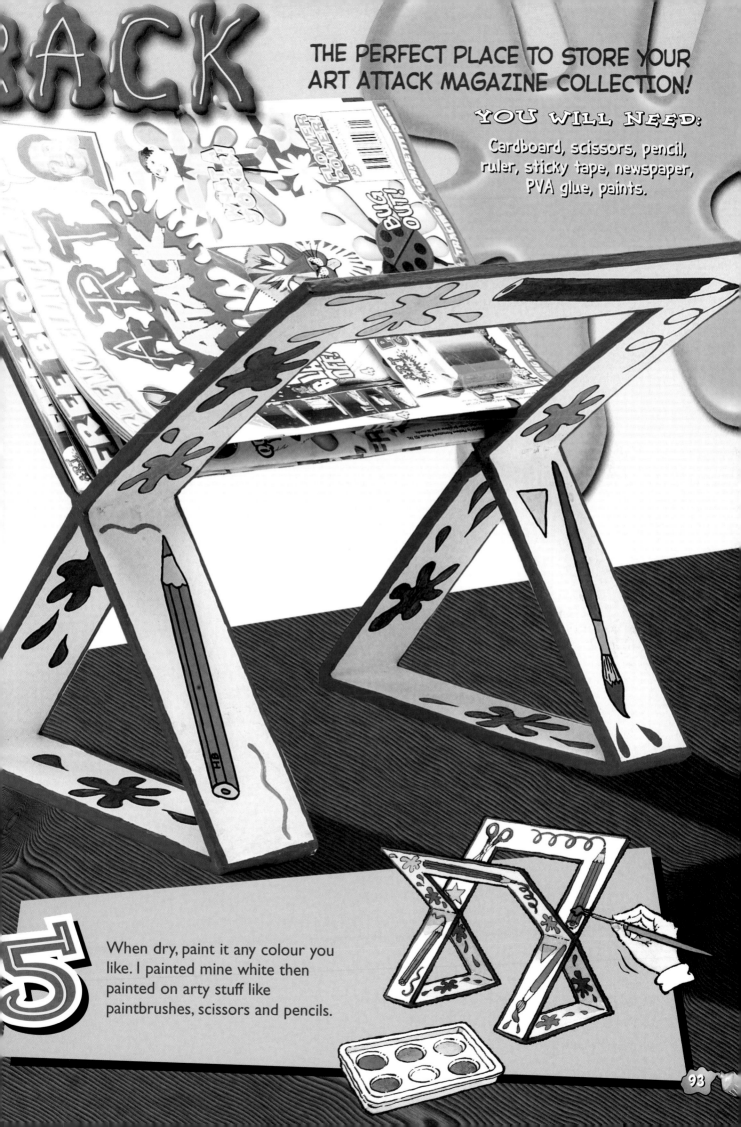

RACK

THE PERFECT PLACE TO STORE YOUR ART ATTACK MAGAZINE COLLECTION!

YOU WILL NEED:

Cardboard, scissors, pencil, ruler, sticky tape, newspaper, PVA glue, paints.

5 When dry, paint it any colour you like. I painted mine white then painted on arty stuff like paintbrushes, scissors and pencils.

HOW TO DR

HOW DO YOU DRAW THINGS FROM ABOVE OR BELOW? TAKE A LOOK AT THESE DRAWINGS FROM A BIRD'S EYE VIEW AND A WORM'S EYE VIEW...

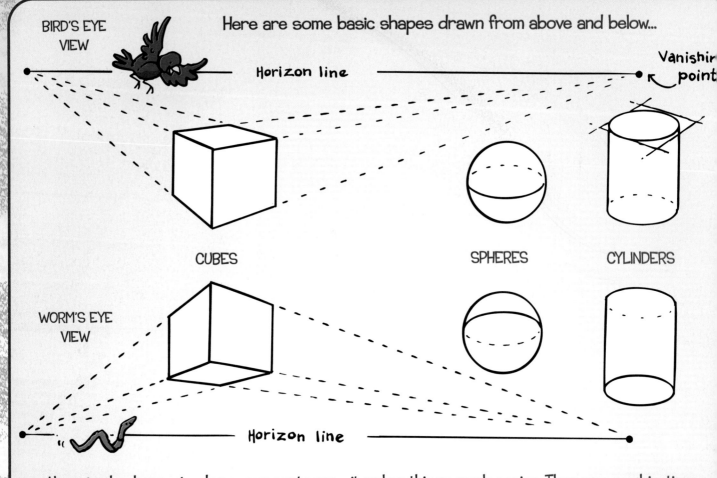

BIRD'S EYE VIEW

Here are some basic shapes drawn from above and below...

Horizon line

Vanishing point

CUBES

SPHERES

CYLINDERS

WORM'S EYE VIEW

Horizon line

Use simple shapes to draw your cartoons - it makes things much easier. Then use combinations of shapes to draw a body from any angle.

W... VIEWPOINTS!

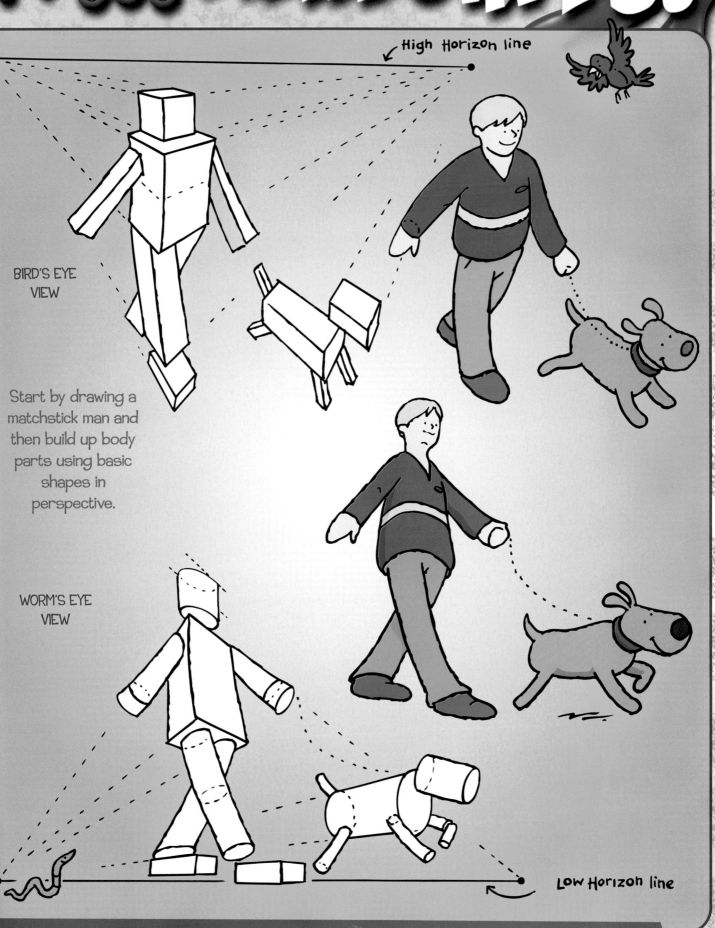

High Horizon line

BIRD'S EYE VIEW

Start by drawing a matchstick man and then build up body parts using basic shapes in perspective.

WORM'S EYE VIEW

Low Horizon line

TURN OVER THE PAGE TO HAVE A GO YOURSELF!

Horizon line

DRAW A BIRD'S EYE VIEW

DRAW A WORM'S EYE VIEW

Horizon line

PLATE FACES!

MAKE SIMPLE MASKS FROM PAPER PLATES. HERE ARE THREE IDEAS, BUT YOU CAN THINK UP SOME OF YOUR OWN!

PUSSY

Cut ears and a triangular nose and glue in place on the plate. Cut holes for the eyes. Paint the plate to look like a cat. Make holes either side and tie some elastic in place.

PIGGY

Cut out a large oval shape and stick it on the front to make a nose, attach two card ears. Paint the plate pink and add some brown patches for mud. Make two holes for eyes. Create a face with black paint and let it dry. Make holes either side, attach elastic and it's ready to wear!

PUPPY

Cut long, oval ears and a nose from card and stick in place. Pierce small holes for your eyes. Paint the plate beige with brown patches. Add details with black paint. Finally make holes either side and thread some elastic through.

ON DISPLAY

THESE SIMPLE DISPLAY FRAMES ARE GREAT FOR SHOWING OFF THINGS YOU HAVE COLLECTED OR YOUR FAVOURITE TOYS. YOU CAN MAKE THEM ANY SIZE YOU LIKE. READ ON TO SEE WHAT TO DO...

Southend-On-Sea
5th August 2000

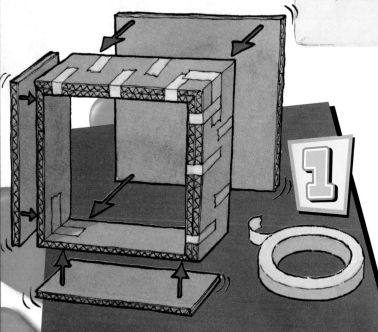

1

Stick thick strips of cardboard together, to make a frame. (Make them as wide as you like - I made mine about 5cm wide.) Add a second layer of strips to make the sides extra thick and a rectangle of card to fit the back.

2

Cover the whole thing with at least three layers of torn newspaper pasted on with diluted PVA glue. Leave it to dry.

IF YOU WANT TO MAKE A REALLY BIG DISPLAY BOX, STRENGTHEN THE CARDBOARD WITH ANOTHER LAYER OF CARD AND COVER IT WITH MORE LAYERS OF PAPIER MACHE.

ART ATTACK

School trip 26-04-01 Hadlow Farm

Southend-On-Sea 5th August 2000

3 Now paint the box. Paint it white all over and leave it to dry. Then paint a picture on the inside - what about a seaside scene or a country landscape?

4 You could use the box to display a special souvenir. What about adding a little label from trimmed card and pinning it to the front of the frame?

99

DESIGN-A-LABELS

MAKE YOUR MARK WITH THESE SUPER COOL LABEL SIMPLY FOLLOW THI STEPS TO G LABELLED...

Victoria
name

David
name

You will need:
scissors, felt tip pens, glue

1 Trace or photocopy the jar labels on the right-hand page. If you photocopy them, you can shrink or enlarge them depending on how big your boxes or jars are.

2 Cut the labels out and then colour them in brightly. Colour the name space in a light colour so you can write in it.

3 Now stick the labels to jars, boxes or anything you want to store things in.

Make lots of labels but instead of writing your name in the space, write what you are collecting. What about stickers, football cards, jewellery, Art Attack bits, whatever?

ATTACK

IF YOU DON'T WANT TO RUIN YOUR ANNUAL, DON'T CUT THEM OUT. ASK AN ADULT TO PHOTOCOPY THIS PAGE FOR YOU INSTEAD.

GET HOOK

HANG AROUND FOR ANOTHER COOL ART ATTACK -
FOLLOW THE STEPS TO CREATE A BRIGHT AND FUN HOOK RACK!

1 Cut a long rectangle from cardboard box card. (If the card is not very thick, stick several layers together.) Carefully cut wave shapes along the top.

2 Cut other shapes from cardboard. I've added a ship and a lighthouse but you could cut out yachts or a mermaid. How about a little island and a palm tree? Stick your shapes on the back of your wave shape.

3 Now cover the waves and shapes with three layers of torn newspaper and diluted PVA glue. Let this dry.

PVA

ED!

Glue on three corks or cut down thin cardboard tubes to make hooks. Cut out three fish shapes from card and stick them onto the ends. Cover with another layer of papier maché. Make sure you keep it neat around the hooks. Let it dry.

5

Finally, you can paint your hook rack. Use bright seaside colours. Let it dry before getting an adult to mount it on your wall. Remember it will only take light items such as school ties or little bags.

SECRET SPELLBOOK

CREATE A SECRET SPELLBOOK HIDEAWAY! THIS ONE IS REALLY MAGIC!

1

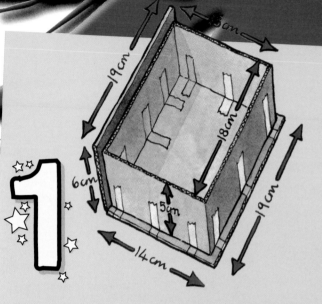

Cut two pieces of card measuring 18cm x 5cm and two, 13cm x 5cm to make the box sides. Cut out two measuring 19cm x 14cm for the front and back and one, 19cm x 6cm for the spine. Assemble the pieces securing them with sticky tape.

2

The front cover should be attached last by sticking it on to the long edge of the spine with strips of paper inside and out, to form a hinge.

3

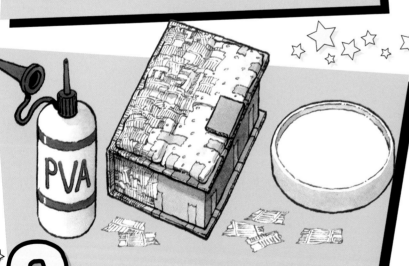

Pad out the front cover with folded paper. Stick on a small square of thick card to make the lock then cover the whole thing with 3 layers of papier maché avoiding the hinge.

4

When dry, paint your spell book. I painted this one dark purple with red corners, lock and lettering. Use a black pen to draw lines along the sides to look like pages.

YOU WILL NEED:

Cardboard, scissors, ruler, pencil, sticky tape, paper, PVA glue, newspaper, tissue paper, paints.

KEEP YOUR SPELLS AND WAND INSIDE YOUR SECRET SPELLBOOK!

5

To make parchment paper, paste small torn squares of tissue paper onto a sheet of thick paper, using diluted PVA glue. When dry, tear the edges, brush with thin yellowy-brown paint before writing a secret spell. Roll up and tie with ribbon.

6

To make a wand, roll up a sheet of paper into a slightly tapered tube. Roll up small balls of paper, stick them on and then cover with 2 layers of papier maché. Paint it to look like wood.

SNOW M...

TO MAKE THIS PICTURE COME ALIVE WE HAVE USED A TECHNIQUE KNOWN AS 'LAYERING'. LAYERING IS THE DECORATION OF SURFACES WITH PAPER CUT OUTS AND CARD TO CREATE A COOL 3D EFFECT.

FUN!

1. Make several photocopies of this picture depending on how many layers you want to make.

2. Stick one of the pictures onto a piece of card, and colour it in. This is your base picture.

3. From the other copies of the picture, decide which bits of the picture you want to raise and cut them out.

4. Looking at your base picture, colour your cut out pieces the same.

5. Cut out small squares of cardboard. Make sure that the card squares are small enough to hide behind the bits of the picture that you want to raise.

6. Stick the little bits of card together, layering them on top of each other. The thicker you make them, the more raised the cut outs will become. Some can be more raised than others.

7. Glue the cardboard onto the base picture and stick the cut out sections on top.

8. Repeat this process with as many different bits of the picture that you want.

THE MORE CARDBOARD THAT YOU STICK TO THE BACK OF THE PIECE YOU HAVE CUT OUT, THE MORE RAISED IT APPEARS.

Bug Out

FOR AN ULTRA-3D EFFECT, CUT SHAPES FROM THICK CARD AND COVER EACH ONE WITH PAPER!

LOOK AT THESE FUNNY, SCARY BUGS! COPY THESE OR MAKE UP YOUR OWN WITH WILD COMBINATIONS OF COLOURS AND THE FUNNIEST FACES!

1) For a body, cut a circle of card and cover it with paper. Add stripes or spots - or both - by sticking on bits of paper in a contrasting colour. Cut a smaller circle or other shape for a head.

2) Stick lengths of pipe cleaners to the back of the bug, for legs and antennae. You can push beads on to the ends of the pipe cleaners, if you like!

3) Glue on goggly eyes, using PVA glue. Stick the bugs to backing card.

Top Tips!

To make the bodies, how about using plastic lids? Use double-sided sticky tape or glue to cover them with coloured paper.

You can decorate your bugs with colourful stickers or you could paint them.

WHAT ABOUT BUGGING SOMEONE ELSE!

Secure some thread to the back of your bug and hang it up - in the fridge, in the car, in a cupboard, in the bathroom cabinet - anywhere you can bug someone!